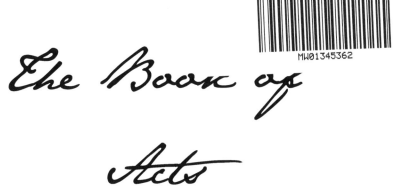

_____

Journal

This time with the Lord journal is a resource from
MissionalWomen.com

© 2015 Laura Krokos
No part of this book may be reproduced or transmitted in any form or by any means, electronic or mechanical, including photocopying and recording, or by any information storage or retrieval system, except as may be expressly permitted.

ISBN-13:978-1542755498

ISBN-10:1542755492

To order additional copies of this resource, order online at
www.MissionalWomen.com

Printed in the United States of America.

Date:

Acts

Chapter One

Before you start, take time to ask the Lord if there is anything you need to confess. If He brings something to mind, confess it and yield your life and heart to Him and ask Him to lead your thinking. Then use the space below to express what's on your mind and heart and submit it to Him.

Read Chapter One
Make note of the things that jump out at you as you read.

Paraphrase
Sum up what you read.

Process
Put yourself in this situation, what would you be thinking and feeling?

What do these verses show you about God's character?

Pursue
Of the verses that jumped out at you look them up in Bible study tools (Commentaries, Strong's, Bible dictionaries etc.) and write down what you learn.
BibleStudyTools.com, BibleHub.com, MyStudyBible.com, BlueLetterBible.com are helpful sites.

Ask God why He brought these things to your mind. Write down the thoughts that come to mind.

Principles
Write down some principles that stick out to you.

1.

2.

3.

Praise
Spend time praising God for who He is and how He has revealed Himself to you.

Personal Application
How does what stood out relate to your personal day to day life? How can you respond with action-oriented faith to what God has brought to your mind?

Pray
Spend some time talking to God about what He showed you, remembering you can do nothing eternal apart from His strength and ability. And spend some time talking to Him about other things on your mind and people and circumstances in your life He brings to mind.

Acts

Chapter Two

Before you start, take time to ask the Lord if there is anything you need to confess. If He brings something to mind, confess it and yield your life and heart to Him and ask Him to lead your thinking. Then use the space below to express what's on your mind and heart and submit it to Him.

Read Chapter Two
Make note of the things that jump out at you as you read.

Paraphrase
Sum up what you read.

Process
Put yourself in this situation, what would you be thinking and feeling?

What do these verses show you about God's character?

Pursue
Of the verses that jumped out at you look them up in Bible study tools (Commentaries, Strong's, Bible dictionaries etc.) and write down what you learn.
BibleStudyTools.com, BibleHub.com, MyStudyBible.com, BlueLetterBible.com are helpful sites.

Ask God why He brought these things to your mind. Write down the thoughts that come to mind.

Principles
Write down some principles that stick out to you.

1.

2.

3.

Praise
Spend time praising God for who He is and how He has revealed Himself to you.

Personal Application
How does what stood out relate to your personal day to day life? How can you respond with action-oriented faith to what God has brought to your mind?

Pray
Spend some time talking to God about what He showed you, remembering you can do nothing eternal apart from His strength and ability. And spend some time talking to Him about other things on your mind and people and circumstances in your life He brings to mind.

Acts

Chapter Three

Before you start, take time to ask the Lord if there is anything you need to confess. If He brings something to mind, confess it and yield your life and heart to Him and ask Him to lead your thinking. Then use the space below to express what's on your mind and heart and submit it to Him.

Read Chapter Three
Make note of the things that jump out at you as you read.

Paraphrase
Sum up what you read.

Process
Put yourself in this situation, what would you be thinking and feeling?

What do these verses show you about God's character?

Pursue
Of the verses that jumped out at you look them up in Bible study tools (Commentaries, Strong's, Bible dictionaries etc.) and write down what you learn.
BibleStudyTools.com, BibleHub.com, MyStudyBible.com, BlueLetterBible.com are helpful sites.

Ask God why He brought these things to your mind. Write down the thoughts that come to mind.

Principles
Write down some principles that stick out to you.

1.

2.

3.

Praise
Spend time praising God for who He is and how He has revealed Himself to you.

Personal Application

How does what stood out relate to your personal day to day life? How can you respond with action-oriented faith to what God has brought to your mind?

Pray

Spend some time talking to God about what He showed you, remembering you can do nothing eternal apart from His strength and ability. And spend some time talking to Him about other things on your mind and people and circumstances in your life He brings to mind.

Acts

Chapter Four

Before you start, take time to ask the Lord if there is anything you need to confess. If He brings something to mind, confess it and yield your life and heart to Him and ask Him to lead your thinking. Then use the space below to express what's on your mind and heart and submit it to Him.

Read Chapter Four
Make note of the things that jump out at you as you read.

Paraphrase
Sum up what you read.

Process
Put yourself in this situation, what would you be thinking and feeling?

What do these verses show you about God's character?

Pursue
Of the verses that jumped out at you look them up in Bible study tools (Commentaries, Strong's, Bible dictionaries etc.) and write down what you learn.
BibleStudyTools.com, BibleHub.com, MyStudyBible.com, BlueLetterBible.com are helpful sites.

Ask God why He brought these things to your mind. Write down the thoughts that come to mind.

Principles
Write down some principles that stick out to you.

1.

2.

3.

Praise
Spend time praising God for who He is and how He has revealed Himself to you.

Personal Application
How does what stood out relate to your personal day to day life? How can you respond with action-oriented faith to what God has brought to your mind?

Pray
Spend some time talking to God about what He showed you, remembering you can do nothing eternal apart from His strength and ability. And spend some time talking to Him about other things on your mind and people and circumstances in your life He brings to mind.

Acts

Chapter Five

Before you start, take time to ask the Lord if there is anything you need to confess. If He brings something to mind, confess it and yield your life and heart to Him and ask Him to lead your thinking. Then use the space below to express what's on your mind and heart and submit it to Him.

Read Chapter Five
Make note of the things that jump out at you as you read.

Paraphrase
Sum up what you read.

Process
Put yourself in this situation, what would you be thinking and feeling?

What do these verses show you about God's character?

Pursue
Of the verses that jumped out at you look them up in Bible study tools (Commentaries, Strong's, Bible dictionaries etc.) and write down what you learn.
BibleStudyTools.com, BibleHub.com, MyStudyBible.com, BlueLetterBible.com are helpful sites.

Ask God why He brought these things to your mind. Write down the thoughts that come to mind.

Principles
Write down some principles that stick out to you.

1.

2.

3.

Praise
Spend time praising God for who He is and how He has revealed Himself to you.

Personal Application
How does what stood out relate to your personal day to day life? How can you respond with action-oriented faith to what God has brought to your mind?

Pray
Spend some time talking to God about what He showed you, remembering you can do nothing eternal apart from His strength and ability. And spend some time talking to Him about other things on your mind and people and circumstances in your life He brings to mind.

Acts

Chapter Six

Before you start, take time to ask the Lord if there is anything you need to confess. If He brings something to mind, confess it and yield your life and heart to Him and ask Him to lead your thinking. Then use the space below to express what's on your mind and heart and submit it to Him.

Read Chapter Six
Make note of the things that jump out at you as you read.

Paraphrase
Sum up what you read.

Process
Put yourself in this situation, what would you be thinking and feeling?

What do these verses show you about God's character?

Pursue
Of the verses that jumped out at you look them up in Bible study tools (Commentaries, Strong's, Bible dictionaries etc.) and write down what you learn.
BibleStudyTools.com, BibleHub.com, MyStudyBible.com, BlueLetterBible.com are helpful sites.

Ask God why He brought these things to your mind. Write down the thoughts that come to mind.

Principles
Write down some principles that stick out to you.

1.

2.

3.

Praise
Spend time praising God for who He is and how He has revealed Himself to you.

Personal Application
How does what stood out relate to your personal day to day life? How can you respond with action-oriented faith to what God has brought to your mind?

Pray
Spend some time talking to God about what He showed you, remembering you can do nothing eternal apart from His strength and ability. And spend some time talking to Him about other things on your mind and people and circumstances in your life He brings to mind.

Acts

Chapter Seven

Before you start, take time to ask the Lord if there is anything you need to confess. If He brings something to mind, confess it and yield your life and heart to Him and ask Him to lead your thinking. Then use the space below to express what's on your mind and heart and submit it to Him.

Read Chapter Seven
Make note of the things that jump out at you as you read.

Paraphrase
Sum up what you read.

Process
Put yourself in this situation, what would you be thinking and feeling?

What do these verses show you about God's character?

Pursue
Of the verses that jumped out at you look them up in Bible study tools (Commentaries, Strong's, Bible dictionaries etc.) and write down what you learn.
BibleStudyTools.com, BibleHub.com, MyStudyBible.com, BlueLetterBible.com are helpful sites.

Ask God why He brought these things to your mind. Write down the thoughts that come to mind.

Principles
Write down some principles that stick out to you.

1.

2.

3.

Praise
Spend time praising God for who He is and how He has revealed Himself to you.

Personal Application
How does what stood out relate to your personal day to day life? How can you respond with action-oriented faith to what God has brought to your mind?

Pray
Spend some time talking to God about what He showed you, remembering you can do nothing eternal apart from His strength and ability. And spend some time talking to Him about other things on your mind and people and circumstances in your life He brings to mind.

Acts

Chapter Eight

Before you start, take time to ask the Lord if there is anything you need to confess. If He brings something to mind, confess it and yield your life and heart to Him and ask Him to lead your thinking. Then use the space below to express what's on your mind and heart and submit it to Him.

Read Chapter Eight
Make note of the things that jump out at you as you read.

Paraphrase
Sum up what you read.

Process
Put yourself in this situation, what would you be thinking and feeling?

What do these verses show you about God's character?

Pursue
Of the verses that jumped out at you look them up in Bible study tools (Commentaries, Strong's, Bible dictionaries etc.) and write down what you learn.
BibleStudyTools.com, BibleHub.com, MyStudyBible.com, BlueLetterBible.com are helpful sites.

Ask God why He brought these things to your mind. Write down the thoughts that come to mind.

Principles
Write down some principles that stick out to you.

1.

2.

3.

Praise
Spend time praising God for who He is and how He has revealed Himself to you.

Personal Application

How does what stood out relate to your personal day to day life? How can you respond with action-oriented faith to what God has brought to your mind?

Pray

Spend some time talking to God about what He showed you, remembering you can do nothing eternal apart from His strength and ability. And spend some time talking to Him about other things on your mind and people and circumstances in your life He brings to mind.

Acts

Chapter Nine

Before you start, take time to ask the Lord if there is anything you need to confess. If He brings something to mind, confess it and yield your life and heart to Him and ask Him to lead your thinking. Then use the space below to express what's on your mind and heart and submit it to Him.

Read Chapter Nine
Make note of the things that jump out at you as you read.

Paraphrase
Sum up what you read.

Process
Put yourself in this situation, what would you be thinking and feeling?

What do these verses show you about God's character?

Pursue
Of the verses that jumped out at you look them up in Bible study tools (Commentaries, Strong's, Bible dictionaries etc.) and write down what you learn.
BibleStudyTools.com, BibleHub.com, MyStudyBible.com, BlueLetterBible.com are helpful sites.

Ask God why He brought these things to your mind. Write down the thoughts that come to mind.

Principles
Write down some principles that stick out to you.

1.

2.

3.

Praise
Spend time praising God for who He is and how He has revealed Himself to you.

Personal Application
How does what stood out relate to your personal day to day life? How can you respond with action-oriented faith to what God has brought to your mind?

Pray
Spend some time talking to God about what He showed you, remembering you can do nothing eternal apart from His strength and ability. And spend some time talking to Him about other things on your mind and people and circumstances in your life He brings to mind.

Acts

Chapter Ten

Before you start, take time to ask the Lord if there is anything you need to confess. If He brings something to mind, confess it and yield your life and heart to Him and ask Him to lead your thinking. Then use the space below to express what's on your mind and heart and submit it to Him.

Read Chapter Ten
Make note of the things that jump out at you as you read.

Paraphrase
Sum up what you read.

Process
Put yourself in this situation, what would you be thinking and feeling?

What do these verses show you about God's character?

Pursue
Of the verses that jumped out at you look them up in Bible study tools (Commentaries, Strong's, Bible dictionaries etc.) and write down what you learn.
BibleStudyTools.com, BibleHub.com, MyStudyBible.com, BlueLetterBible.com are helpful sites.

Ask God why He brought these things to your mind. Write down the thoughts that come to mind.

Principles
Write down some principles that stick out to you.

1.

2.

3.

Praise
Spend time praising God for who He is and how He has revealed Himself to you.

Personal Application
How does what stood out relate to your personal day to day life? How can you respond with action-oriented faith to what God has brought to your mind?

Pray
Spend some time talking to God about what He showed you, remembering you can do nothing eternal apart from His strength and ability. And spend some time talking to Him about other things on your mind and people and circumstances in your life He brings to mind.

Acts

Chapter Eleven

Before you start, take time to ask the Lord if there is anything you need to confess. If He brings something to mind, confess it and yield your life and heart to Him and ask Him to lead your thinking. Then use the space below to express what's on your mind and heart and submit it to Him.

Read Chapter Eleven
Make note of the things that jump out at you as you read.

Paraphrase
Sum up what you read.

Process
Put yourself in this situation, what would you be thinking and feeling?

What do these verses show you about God's character?

Pursue
Of the verses that jumped out at you look them up in Bible study tools (Commentaries, Strong's, Bible dictionaries etc.) and write down what you learn.
BibleStudyTools.com, BibleHub.com, MyStudyBible.com, BlueLetterBible.com are helpful sites.

Ask God why He brought these things to your mind. Write down the thoughts that come to mind.

Principles
Write down some principles that stick out to you.

1.

2.

3.

Praise
Spend time praising God for who He is and how He has revealed Himself to you.

Personal Application
How does what stood out relate to your personal day to day life? How can you respond with action-oriented faith to what God has brought to your mind?

Pray
Spend some time talking to God about what He showed you, remembering you can do nothing eternal apart from His strength and ability. And spend some time talking to Him about other things on your mind and people and circumstances in your life He brings to mind.

Acts

Chapter Twelve

Before you start, take time to ask the Lord if there is anything you need to confess. If He brings something to mind, confess it and yield your life and heart to Him and ask Him to lead your thinking. Then use the space below to express what's on your mind and heart and submit it to Him.

Read Chapter Twelve
Make note of the things that jump out at you as you read.

Paraphrase
Sum up what you read.

Process
Put yourself in this situation, what would you be thinking and feeling?

What do these verses show you about God's character?

Pursue
Of the verses that jumped out at you look them up in Bible study tools (Commentaries, Strong's, Bible dictionaries etc.) and write down what you learn.
BibleStudyTools.com, BibleHub.com, MyStudyBible.com, BlueLetterBible.com are helpful sites.

Ask God why He brought these things to your mind. Write down the thoughts that come to mind.

Principles
Write down some principles that stick out to you.

1.

2.

3.

Praise
Spend time praising God for who He is and how He has revealed Himself to you.

Personal Application
How does what stood out relate to your personal day to day life? How can you respond with action-oriented faith to what God has brought to your mind?

Pray
Spend some time talking to God about what He showed you, remembering you can do nothing eternal apart from His strength and ability. And spend some time talking to Him about other things on your mind and people and circumstances in your life He brings to mind.

Acts

Chapter Thirteen

Before you start, take time to ask the Lord if there is anything you need to confess. If He brings something to mind, confess it and yield your life and heart to Him and ask Him to lead your thinking. Then use the space below to express what's on your mind and heart and submit it to Him.

Read Chapter Thirteen
Make note of the things that jump out at you as you read.

Paraphrase
Sum up what you read.

Process
Put yourself in this situation, what would you be thinking and feeling?

What do these verses show you about God's character?

Pursue
Of the verses that jumped out at you look them up in Bible study tools (Commentaries, Strong's, Bible dictionaries etc.) and write down what you learn.
BibleStudyTools.com, BibleHub.com, MyStudyBible.com, BlueLetterBible.com are helpful sites.

Ask God why He brought these things to your mind. Write down the thoughts that come to mind.

Principles
Write down some principles that stick out to you.

1.

2.

3.

Praise
Spend time praising God for who He is and how He has revealed Himself to you.

Personal Application
How does what stood out relate to your personal day to day life? How can you respond with action-oriented faith to what God has brought to your mind?

Pray
Spend some time talking to God about what He showed you, remembering you can do nothing eternal apart from His strength and ability. And spend some time talking to Him about other things on your mind and people and circumstances in your life He brings to mind.

Acts

Chapter Fourteen

Before you start, take time to ask the Lord if there is anything you need to confess. If He brings something to mind, confess it and yield your life and heart to Him and ask Him to lead your thinking. Then use the space below to express what's on your mind and heart and submit it to Him.

Read Chapter Fourteen
Make note of the things that jump out at you as you read.

Paraphrase
Sum up what you read.

Process
Put yourself in this situation, what would you be thinking and feeling?

What do these verses show you about God's character?

Pursue
Of the verses that jumped out at you look them up in Bible study tools (Commentaries, Strong's, Bible dictionaries etc.) and write down what you learn.
BibleStudyTools.com, BibleHub.com, MyStudyBible.com, BlueLetterBible.com are helpful sites.

Ask God why He brought these things to your mind. Write down the thoughts that come to mind.

Principles
Write down some principles that stick out to you.

1.

2.

3.

Praise
Spend time praising God for who He is and how He has revealed Himself to you.

Personal Application
How does what stood out relate to your personal day to day life? How can you respond with action-oriented faith to what God has brought to your mind?

Pray
Spend some time talking to God about what He showed you, remembering you can do nothing eternal apart from His strength and ability. And spend some time talking to Him about other things on your mind and people and circumstances in your life He brings to mind.

Acts

Chapter Fifteen

Before you start, take time to ask the Lord if there is anything you need to confess. If He brings something to mind, confess it and yield your life and heart to Him and ask Him to lead your thinking. Then use the space below to express what's on your mind and heart and submit it to Him.

Read Chapter Fifteen
Make note of the things that jump out at you as you read.

Paraphrase
Sum up what you read.

Process
Put yourself in this situation, what would you be thinking and feeling?

What do these verses show you about God's character?

Pursue
Of the verses that jumped out at you look them up in Bible study tools (Commentaries, Strong's, Bible dictionaries etc.) and write down what you learn.
BibleStudyTools.com, BibleHub.com, MyStudyBible.com, BlueLetterBible.com are helpful sites.

Ask God why He brought these things to your mind. Write down the thoughts that come to mind.

Principles
Write down some principles that stick out to you.

1.

2.

3.

Praise
Spend time praising God for who He is and how He has revealed Himself to you.

Personal Application

How does what stood out relate to your personal day to day life? How can you respond with action-oriented faith to what God has brought to your mind?

Pray

Spend some time talking to God about what He showed you, remembering you can do nothing eternal apart from His strength and ability. And spend some time talking to Him about other things on your mind and people and circumstances in your life He brings to mind.

Acts

Chapter Sixteen

Before you start, take time to ask the Lord if there is anything you need to confess. If He brings something to mind, confess it and yield your life and heart to Him and ask Him to lead your thinking. Then use the space below to express what's on your mind and heart and submit it to Him.

Read Chapter Sixteen
Make note of the things that jump out at you as you read.

Paraphrase
Sum up what you read.

Process
Put yourself in this situation, what would you be thinking and feeling?

What do these verses show you about God's character?

Pursue
Of the verses that jumped out at you look them up in Bible study tools (Commentaries, Strong's, Bible dictionaries etc.) and write down what you learn.
BibleStudyTools.com, BibleHub.com, MyStudyBible.com, BlueLetterBible.com are helpful sites.

Ask God why He brought these things to your mind. Write down the thoughts that come to mind.

Principles
Write down some principles that stick out to you.

1.

2.

3.

Praise
Spend time praising God for who He is and how He has revealed Himself to you.

Personal Application
How does what stood out relate to your personal day to day life? How can you respond with action-oriented faith to what God has brought to your mind?

Pray
Spend some time talking to God about what He showed you, remembering you can do nothing eternal apart from His strength and ability. And spend some time talking to Him about other things on your mind and people and circumstances in your life He brings to mind.

Acts

Chapter Seventeen

Before you start, take time to ask the Lord if there is anything you need to confess. If He brings something to mind, confess it and yield your life and heart to Him and ask Him to lead your thinking. Then use the space below to express what's on your mind and heart and submit it to Him.

Read Chapter Seventeen
Make note of the things that jump out at you as you read.

Paraphrase
Sum up what you read.

Process
Put yourself in this situation, what would you be thinking and feeling?

What do these verses show you about God's character?

Pursue
Of the verses that jumped out at you look them up in Bible study tools (Commentaries, Strong's, Bible dictionaries etc.) and write down what you learn.
BibleStudyTools.com, BibleHub.com, MyStudyBible.com, BlueLetterBible.com are helpful sites.

Ask God why He brought these things to your mind. Write down the thoughts that come to mind.

Principles
Write down some principles that stick out to you.

1.

2.

3.

Praise
Spend time praising God for who He is and how He has revealed Himself to you.

Personal Application
How does what stood out relate to your personal day to day life? How can you respond with action-oriented faith to what God has brought to your mind?

Pray
Spend some time talking to God about what He showed you, remembering you can do nothing eternal apart from His strength and ability. And spend some time talking to Him about other things on your mind and people and circumstances in your life He brings to mind.

Acts

Chapter Eighteen

Before you start, take time to ask the Lord if there is anything you need to confess. If He brings something to mind, confess it and yield your life and heart to Him and ask Him to lead your thinking. Then use the space below to express what's on your mind and heart and submit it to Him.

Read Chapter Eighteen
Make note of the things that jump out at you as you read.

Paraphrase
Sum up what you read.

Process
Put yourself in this situation, what would you be thinking and feeling?

What do these verses show you about God's character?

Pursue
Of the verses that jumped out at you look them up in Bible study tools (Commentaries, Strong's, Bible dictionaries etc.) and write down what you learn.
BibleStudyTools.com, BibleHub.com, MyStudyBible.com, BlueLetterBible.com are helpful sites.

Ask God why He brought these things to your mind. Write down the thoughts that come to mind.

Principles
Write down some principles that stick out to you.

1.

2.

3.

Praise
Spend time praising God for who He is and how He has revealed Himself to you.

Personal Application
How does what stood out relate to your personal day to day life? How can you respond with action-oriented faith to what God has brought to your mind?

Pray
Spend some time talking to God about what He showed you, remembering you can do nothing eternal apart from His strength and ability. And spend some time talking to Him about other things on your mind and people and circumstances in your life He brings to mind.

Acts

Chapter Nineteen

Before you start, take time to ask the Lord if there is anything you need to confess. If He brings something to mind, confess it and yield your life and heart to Him and ask Him to lead your thinking. Then use the space below to express what's on your mind and heart and submit it to Him.

Read Chapter Nineteen

Make note of the things that jump out at you as you read.

Paraphrase
Sum up what you read.

Process
Put yourself in this situation, what would you be thinking and feeling?

What do these verses show you about God's character?

Pursue
Of the verses that jumped out at you look them up in Bible study tools (Commentaries, Strong's, Bible dictionaries etc.) and write down what you learn.
BibleStudyTools.com, BibleHub.com, MyStudyBible.com, BlueLetterBible.com are helpful sites.

Ask God why He brought these things to your mind. Write down the thoughts that come to mind.

Principles
Write down some principles that stick out to you.

1.

2.

3.

Praise
Spend time praising God for who He is and how He has revealed Himself to you.

Personal Application
How does what stood out relate to your personal day to day life? How can you respond with action-oriented faith to what God has brought to your mind?

Pray
Spend some time talking to God about what He showed you, remembering you can do nothing eternal apart from His strength and ability. And spend some time talking to Him about other things on your mind and people and circumstances in your life He brings to mind.

Acts

Chapter Twenty

Before you start, take time to ask the Lord if there is anything you need to confess. If He brings something to mind, confess it and yield your life and heart to Him and ask Him to lead your thinking. Then use the space below to express what's on your mind and heart and submit it to Him.

Read Chapter Twenty
Make note of the things that jump out at you as you read.

Paraphrase
Sum up what you read.

Process
Put yourself in this situation, what would you be thinking and feeling?

What do these verses show you about God's character?

Pursue
Of the verses that jumped out at you look them up in Bible study tools (Commentaries, Strong's, Bible dictionaries etc.) and write down what you learn.
BibleStudyTools.com, BibleHub.com, MyStudyBible.com, BlueLetterBible.com are helpful sites.

Ask God why He brought these things to your mind. Write down the thoughts that come to mind.

Principles
Write down some principles that stick out to you.

1.

2.

3.

Praise
Spend time praising God for who He is and how He has revealed Himself to you.

Personal Application
How does what stood out relate to your personal day to day life? How can you respond with action-oriented faith to what God has brought to your mind?

Pray
Spend some time talking to God about what He showed you, remembering you can do nothing eternal apart from His strength and ability. And spend some time talking to Him about other things on your mind and people and circumstances in your life He brings to mind.

Acts

Chapter Twenty One

Before you start, take time to ask the Lord if there is anything you need to confess. If He brings something to mind, confess it and yield your life and heart to Him and ask Him to lead your thinking. Then use the space below to express what's on your mind and heart and submit it to Him.

Read Chapter Twenty One
Make note of the things that jump out at you as you read.

Paraphrase
Sum up what you read.

Process
Put yourself in this situation, what would you be thinking and feeling?

What do these verses show you about God's character?

Pursue
Of the verses that jumped out at you look them up in Bible study tools (Commentaries, Strong's, Bible dictionaries etc.) and write down what you learn.
BibleStudyTools.com, BibleHub.com, MyStudyBible.com, BlueLetterBible.com are helpful sites.

Ask God why He brought these things to your mind. Write down the thoughts that come to mind.

Principles
Write down some principles that stick out to you.

1.

2.

3.

Praise
Spend time praising God for who He is and how He has revealed Himself to you.

Personal Application
How does what stood out relate to your personal day to day life? How can you respond with action-oriented faith to what God has brought to your mind?

Pray
Spend some time talking to God about what He showed you, remembering you can do nothing eternal apart from His strength and ability. And spend some time talking to Him about other things on your mind and people and circumstances in your life He brings to mind.

Acts

Chapter Twenty Two

Before you start, take time to ask the Lord if there is anything you need to confess. If He brings something to mind, confess it and yield your life and heart to Him and ask Him to lead your thinking. Then use the space below to express what's on your mind and heart and submit it to Him.

Read Chapter Twenty Two
Make note of the things that jump out at you as you read.

Paraphrase
Sum up what you read.

Process
Put yourself in this situation, what would you be thinking and feeling?

What do these verses show you about God's character?

Pursue
Of the verses that jumped out at you look them up in Bible study tools (Commentaries, Strong's, Bible dictionaries etc.) and write down what you learn.
BibleStudyTools.com, BibleHub.com, MyStudyBible.com, BlueLetterBible.com are helpful sites.

Ask God why He brought these things to your mind. Write down the thoughts that come to mind.

Principles
Write down some principles that stick out to you.

1.

2.

3.

Praise
Spend time praising God for who He is and how He has revealed Himself to you.

Personal Application
How does what stood out relate to your personal day to day life? How can you respond with action-oriented faith to what God has brought to your mind?

Pray
Spend some time talking to God about what He showed you, remembering you can do nothing eternal apart from His strength and ability. And spend some time talking to Him about other things on your mind and people and circumstances in your life He brings to mind.

Acts

Chapter Twenty Three

Before you start, take time to ask the Lord if there is anything you need to confess. If He brings something to mind, confess it and yield your life and heart to Him and ask Him to lead your thinking. Then use the space below to express what's on your mind and heart and submit it to Him.

Read Chapter Twenty Three
Make note of the things that jump out at you as you read.

Paraphrase
Sum up what you read.

Process
Put yourself in this situation, what would you be thinking and feeling?

What do these verses show you about God's character?

Pursue
Of the verses that jumped out at you look them up in Bible study tools (Commentaries, Strong's, Bible dictionaries etc.) and write down what you learn.
BibleStudyTools.com, BibleHub.com, MyStudyBible.com, BlueLetterBible.com are helpful sites.

Ask God why He brought these things to your mind. Write down the thoughts that come to mind.

Principles
Write down some principles that stick out to you.

1.

2.

3.

Praise
Spend time praising God for who He is and how He has revealed Himself to you.

Personal Application

How does what stood out relate to your personal day to day life? How can you respond with action-oriented faith to what God has brought to your mind?

Pray

Spend some time talking to God about what He showed you, remembering you can do nothing eternal apart from His strength and ability. And spend some time talking to Him about other things on your mind and people and circumstances in your life He brings to mind.

Acts

Chapter Twenty Four

Before you start, take time to ask the Lord if there is anything you need to confess. If He brings something to mind, confess it and yield your life and heart to Him and ask Him to lead your thinking. Then use the space below to express what's on your mind and heart and submit it to Him.

Read Chapter Twenty Four
Make note of the things that jump out at you as you read.

Paraphrase
Sum up what you read.

Process
Put yourself in this situation, what would you be thinking and feeling?

What do these verses show you about God's character?

Pursue
Of the verses that jumped out at you look them up in Bible study tools (Commentaries, Strong's, Bible dictionaries etc.) and write down what you learn.
BibleStudyTools.com, BibleHub.com, MyStudyBible.com, BlueLetterBible.com are helpful sites.

Ask God why He brought these things to your mind. Write down the thoughts that come to mind.

Principles
Write down some principles that stick out to you.

1.

2.

3.

Praise
Spend time praising God for who He is and how He has revealed Himself to you.

Personal Application
How does what stood out relate to your personal day to day life? How can you respond with action-oriented faith to what God has brought to your mind?

Pray
Spend some time talking to God about what He showed you, remembering you can do nothing eternal apart from His strength and ability. And spend some time talking to Him about other things on your mind and people and circumstances in your life He brings to mind.

Acts

Chapter Twenty Five

Before you start, take time to ask the Lord if there is anything you need to confess. If He brings something to mind, confess it and yield your life and heart to Him and ask Him to lead your thinking. Then use the space below to express what's on your mind and heart and submit it to Him.

Read Chapter Twenty Five
Make note of the things that jump out at you as you read.

Paraphrase
Sum up what you read.

Process
Put yourself in this situation, what would you be thinking and feeling?

What do these verses show you about God's character?

Pursue
Of the verses that jumped out at you look them up in Bible study tools (Commentaries, Strong's, Bible dictionaries etc.) and write down what you learn.
BibleStudyTools.com, BibleHub.com, MyStudyBible.com, BlueLetterBible.com are helpful sites.

Ask God why He brought these things to your mind. Write down the thoughts that come to mind.

Principles
Write down some principles that stick out to you.

1.

2.

3.

Praise
Spend time praising God for who He is and how He has revealed Himself to you.

Personal Application
How does what stood out relate to your personal day to day life? How can you respond with action-oriented faith to what God has brought to your mind?

Pray
Spend some time talking to God about what He showed you, remembering you can do nothing eternal apart from His strength and ability. And spend some time talking to Him about other things on your mind and people and circumstances in your life He brings to mind.

Acts

Chapter Twenty Six

Before you start, take time to ask the Lord if there is anything you need to confess. If He brings something to mind, confess it and yield your life and heart to Him and ask Him to lead your thinking. Then use the space below to express what's on your mind and heart and submit it to Him.

Read Chapter Twenty Six
Make note of the things that jump out at you as you read.

Paraphrase
Sum up what you read.

Process
Put yourself in this situation, what would you be thinking and feeling?

What do these verses show you about God's character?

Pursue
Of the verses that jumped out at you look them up in Bible study tools (Commentaries, Strong's, Bible dictionaries etc.) and write down what you learn.
BibleStudyTools.com, BibleHub.com, MyStudyBible.com, BlueLetterBible.com are helpful sites.

Ask God why He brought these things to your mind. Write down the thoughts that come to mind.

Principles
Write down some principles that stick out to you.

1.

2.

3.

Praise
Spend time praising God for who He is and how He has revealed Himself to you.

Personal Application
How does what stood out relate to your personal day to day life? How can you respond with action-oriented faith to what God has brought to your mind?

Pray
Spend some time talking to God about what He showed you, remembering you can do nothing eternal apart from His strength and ability. And spend some time talking to Him about other things on your mind and people and circumstances in your life He brings to mind.

Acts

Chapter Twenty Seven

Before you start, take time to ask the Lord if there is anything you need to confess. If He brings something to mind, confess it and yield your life and heart to Him and ask Him to lead your thinking. Then use the space below to express what's on your mind and heart and submit it to Him.

Read Chapter Twenty Seven
Make note of the things that jump out at you as you read.

Paraphrase
Sum up what you read.

Process
Put yourself in this situation, what would you be thinking and feeling?

What do these verses show you about God's character?

Pursue
Of the verses that jumped out at you look them up in Bible study tools (Commentaries, Strong's, Bible dictionaries etc.) and write down what you learn.
BibleStudyTools.com, BibleHub.com, MyStudyBible.com, BlueLetterBible.com are helpful sites.

Ask God why He brought these things to your mind. Write down the thoughts that come to mind.

Principles
Write down some principles that stick out to you.

1.

2.

3.

Praise
Spend time praising God for who He is and how He has revealed Himself to you.

Personal Application

How does what stood out relate to your personal day to day life? How can you respond with action-oriented faith to what God has brought to your mind?

Pray

Spend some time talking to God about what He showed you, remembering you can do nothing eternal apart from His strength and ability. And spend some time talking to Him about other things on your mind and people and circumstances in your life He brings to mind.

Acts

Chapter Twenty Eight

Before you start, take time to ask the Lord if there is anything you need to confess. If He brings something to mind, confess it and yield your life and heart to Him and ask Him to lead your thinking. Then use the space below to express what's on your mind and heart and submit it to Him.

Read Chapter Twenty Eight
Make note of the things that jump out at you as you read.

Paraphrase
Sum up what you read.

Process
Put yourself in this situation, what would you be thinking and feeling?

What do these verses show you about God's character?

Pursue
Of the verses that jumped out at you look them up in Bible study tools (Commentaries, Strong's, Bible dictionaries etc.) and write down what you learn.
BibleStudyTools.com, BibleHub.com, MyStudyBible.com, BlueLetterBible.com are helpful sites.

Ask God why He brought these things to your mind. Write down the thoughts that come to mind.

Principles
Write down some principles that stick out to you.

1.

2.

3.

Praise
Spend time praising God for who He is and how He has revealed Himself to you.

Personal Application
How does what stood out relate to your personal day to day life? How can you respond with action-oriented faith to what God has brought to your mind?

Pray
Spend some time talking to God about what He showed you, remembering you can do nothing eternal apart from His strength and ability. And spend some time talking to Him about other things on your mind and people and circumstances in your life He brings to mind.

Order your next Journal

Order your next journal at MissionalWomen.com at a 10% discount with the code **nextjournal**

About the Author

Laura is married and has six kids, two of whom are adopted. Laura and her husband have been missionaries to college students for fourteen years where she serves as the Women's Development Coordinator with Master Plan Ministries. She has discipled over two hundred women, led over forty Bible studies and speaks to college and women's groups. Laura is the Founder of the internationally popular blog MissionalWomen.com and has authored five books, including an award winning twelve week Bible Study on First Samuel, *Beholding Him, Becoming Missional, Reach; How to Use Your Social Media Influence for the Glory of God*, and *A Devotional Journey through Judges*.

Other books & resources by Laura

All resources found at MissionalWomen.com

A Creative, Interactive Resource for Small Group Leaders
Deeper connections are critical to a Small Group and creating them can be a challenge. So here is a resource—creative ideas and content—to help your Small Group make those connections.

Why Connect Cards?
Small groups provide an atmosphere where great growth can take place but it takes intentionality to think through how to help group members connect with God, each other and the Great Commission in a deep and meaningful way. **The Connect Cards** provide training, questions and ideas to ensure each of these elements are present each week to make not only a deep and meaningful group but also an influential one.

How it Works
The Connect Cards deck has four essential elements: Connect with Scripture (for the leader), Connect with God (prayer), Connect with Each Other (group interaction), and Connect with The Mission (ministry). There are eleven cards per section, with forty-four cards total.

Each week during your small group Bible Study, chose one card from each section. (There are eleven cards per section) All four categories combined (depending on the size of your group) should last about 30-45 minutes to your group time. If you are short on time, you can do one or two cards a week to go through or you can choose to go through one section/card at a time.

Tailor fit this creative deck to fit your group.

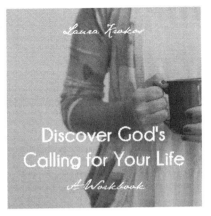

Knowing your calling will help you live a confident, effective life that please the Lord. The content and questions in this workbook will help you know what God desires of your life and by the end of this workbook you will have a clearly defined calling by which to measure all your activity in this life and practical goals to begin (or continue) to walk out the calling the Lord has for you.

Practical, insightful and relatable 250 page in depth devotional study with great personal stories. Each day is short enough to be able to read and have time to process the personal application questions. It can be used in conjunction with the discussion guide (at www.TheBookofJudges.com) or as a standalone devotional.

Customer Reviews
Brilliantly done devotional!

In the Christian literary world there are devotionals and there are Bible studies, and then there is Laura Krokos' A Devotional Journey Through Judges, which is a little bit of both! Her title is apt, as this book truly is a journey. Unlike most devotionals that contain random verses from different parts of the Bible, Journey Through Judges provides consecutive verses beginning at the first verse of Judges and ending with the last, giving the reader a cohesive theme to follow throughout the devotional. The reader is able to gain knowledge of the book of Judges while benefitting from Laura's insight and personal tidbits. I am thoroughly enjoying this devotional. I would recommend it to anyone wanting a devotional that is a bit different from the traditional coffee table edition, or anyone that would like a Bible study that does not require much time. She did a beautiful job on this book! Great work! -Shara Nelson

Made in the USA
Columbia, SC
28 March 2018